The Life and Times of
José Calderon

also by José Faus

This Town Like That
(Spartan Press 2016)

The Life and Times of
José Calderon

poems by
José Faus

39 WEST PRESS

39 WEST PRESS
Kansas City, MO
www.39WestPress.com

39 WEST
PRESS

Copyright © 2017 by José Faus

All rights reserved. No part of this book may be reproduced, scanned, or distributed in any printed or electronic form, including information storage and retrieval systems, without permission. Please do not participate in or encourage piracy of copyrighted materials in violation of the author's rights. Please purchase only authorized editions.

First Edition: May 2017

ISBN: 978-0-9908649-8-1

Library of Congress Control Number: 2016953095

This book is a work of fiction. Names, characters, places, dates, and incidents are products of the author's imagination, or are used fictitiously, satirically, or as parody. Any resemblance to actual persons, living or dead, business establishments, events, or locales is entirely coincidental.

10 9 8 7 6 5 4 3 2 1

Design, Layout, Edits: j.d.tulloch
Front Cover Watercolor & Back Cover/Interior Bull: Chico Sierra
Interior Chapter Heading Illustrations: José Faus

39WP-21

CONTENTS

Foreword
The Life and Times of José Calderon
0) Imagina — 3

Chapter I
José Calderon Supposes

1) José Calderon Supposes — 7
2) A Question Takes Hold — 9
3) Dust in the Corners — 12
4) She Weaves the Shirt — 13
5) Enrique Calderon Painted Pictures — 15
6) His Descent Is a Casual Thing — 17

Chapter II
Border Crossings

7) Border Crossings — 21
8) Family Portrait — 23
9) I Remember Jackson Mississippi — 25
10) The Old House on the Line — 27

Chapter III
This Is Tango

11) This Is Tango — 31
12) How Strange the Night — 33
13) In the Bay — 34
14) One — 35
15) I Enjoy — 36
16) She Is Late Returning — 39
17) Today — 41
18) Amor — 42
19) Rain Will Come What May — 43
20) You Woke Me — 44
21) When the Wind Is Slight — 45

Chapter IV
At the Water's Edge

22) At the Water's Edge — 49
23) In the Simplest of Ways — 51
24) There Is Nothing To Be Found — 53
25) The Water Moves in Circles about My Speech — 54
26) Why I Don't Sing — 60
27) Baile — 62

Chapter V
José Calderon Speaks

28) When I Talk — 67
29) Mood with No Face — 68
30) Fall Is a Craving — 69
31) Ten Days Now without Rest — 71
32) Malvern Hill — 73
33) This Town Like That — 77
34) What Was of Us — 80
35) I Was Mute — 82

Chapter VI
Bitter Suite

36) Bitter Suite — 87

Afterword
The Life and Times of José Calderon

37) Epifania — 103
38) Epilogue — 105

Foreword

The Life and Times of José Calderon

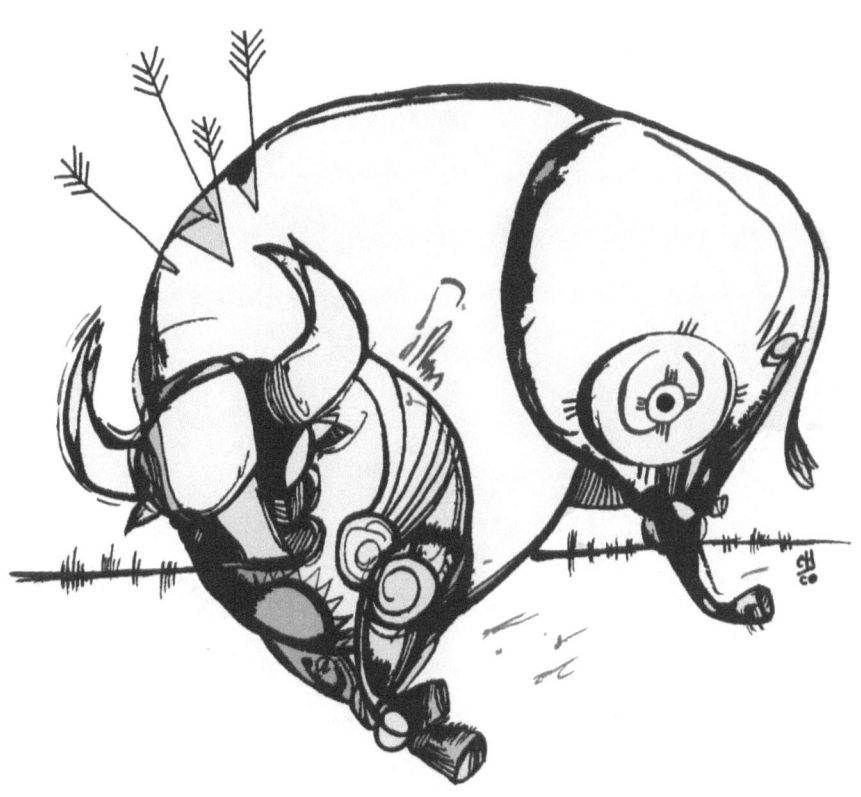

0) *Imagina*

José Calderon walks to the market in the small town above the hills that fold along the river. A gypsy woman sees him enter from Avenida Bolivar with his distant gait and measured gaze. Immediately, she ties her scrawny self to his tall frame and follows him, pestering him, demanding he come to her table.

To drive her away, he asks where her stall stands and promises to visit the minute he finishes his shopping. He is certain the look the woman gives him, as she slowly releases his hand, is the force that draws him back from the outer edge of the market. He takes a deep breath and walks to the far corner of the weathered stalls where the woman waits for him.

She welcomes him and pours jasmine tea into a misshaped ceramic cup. He does not speak but takes slow sips of the fragrant tea while she winks and smiles.

"I'll tell you something," she said. "I'm going to give you a gift because you are one of the few that have ever followed through on their word. That is a great accomplishment. I know you have wondered if there have ever been such moments of grace in your life."

The truth is he has not thought much about his life until that moment, and suddenly, a burdensome loneliness embraces him and makes him shudder in his seat.

"There, there," she tells him, gently patting the back of his hands, which now rest on the table with the empty cup of tea in between, while his eyes dart about the market. He notices all the strangers: the butcher with his haggard smile, the facile look of the herb vendor, the curious stare of the fishmongers, and the cautious gaze of the fruit sellers with one eye on the produce and many eyes on the hands of strangers and friends casually passing by.

"Imagine it is a day like no other day," she tells him. "The sun has never been more gracious. The smiles of strangers as they greet you are a warm caress that rivals the breezes. Imagine your companion weaves the moon's rays into a warm pillow she shares with you at night.

"Imagine you are in the middle of this life. Imagine you are the protagonist. It is your life. Imagine you missed it. There wasn't a distraction. You just never thought to catalogue every moment. Whether big or small, they carried the same load."

She continues, "It's not indifference. You cared deeply ... and often much to your discomfort. But this happens. Imagine a life where Monday is Sunday and worship is like the umbrella by the door. Just make sure it opens when the rain falls.

"Imagine this is not your life – this is not what you wanted or planned," she implores. "But you never thought much about it, much less took the time to plan it. It just happened to you. You ask, somewhere in all the muted colors, was there a shining moment? Must there have been many moments worthy of a book?"

He thinks back to the memories stuffed in the closed drawers of his mind. The tear that escapes down his brown cheek falls into the empty cup. He winces as if the sound of the drop hitting the ceramic void is an enormous wave crashing on the stone cliffs of a town he visited many times when he was a boy.

"Everyone has a book in them," she tells him. "Imagine this is that book."

He looks at her ... notices her withered face, her frail hands, but the spark of her eyes belies her age. It is a young girl's smile. He is hardly aware of the package she puts into his hands.

"Take this and go. You have a lot to write," she commands as she rises slowly from the wicker seat. Touching her hand to his hand, she sighs and turns. She pulls back the curtain of the shack and steps into the darkness.

Chapter 1
José Calderon Supposes

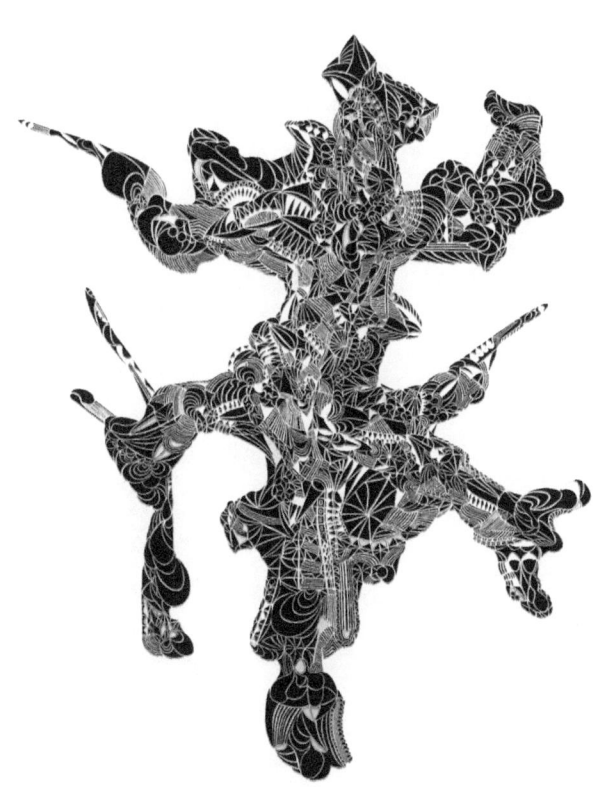

1) José Calderon Supposes

On the fiftieth year of his life
José Calderon buys a set
of black moleskin notebooks
a feather quill relic pen
and a set of professional
calligraphy inks

He climbs the three sets of stairs
to the attic newly converted
into a writing garret

He sits at the desk near the open window
facing out onto the street below
and dutifully removes the plastic foil
from the pack of notebooks
He arranges them on the sparse desk
opens the first page creases it back
lays it flat on the table top
He dips the quill into the inkwell
and sets about to write
the profound arc of his life

Twenty minutes later
the ink dries on the nib
He moves away from profundity
searches the significant achievements
that are his life's narrative
An hour later
he ponders the absurd moments
that surely fill his fifty years

Two hours later
he watches the dogs
chase their tails in the neighbor's yard
watches the squirrels jump into the streets

and at the slightest sound freeze
turn in stutters before returning
where they began or proceeding
to where they meant to go

He watches the play
of hundreds of swifts
diving off the power lines
marvels at the well-played dance
of dips and swoops and plunges
the orchestrated sudden stops and turns
a set of convulsing elastic bands
stretching and pulling away from a center
and springing back to pull away again

An hour later he opens his eyes
and lifts his head from
the sweater covered arm
that has become his rest
He feels the weave of the sweater
etched across his face
sees the sun in its last descent
He looks at the blank page
and begins to write
Seconds later the quill on its rest
he rises abruptly
walks to the door steps out
and closes it behind him

In the room on the desk
across the top of the page
a name written clearly
in block letters fades
in the dim evening light

2) A Question Takes Hold

He watches the race
up the sides of Mount Ventoux
The bikes swinging back and forth
one brother taking charge
pulling the other to the top
while pressed by the Spaniard in yellow
and the survivor in tandem
responding to every break and feint
And he marvels at such a climb
the will to exhaustion for a summit
one could walk leisurely in a day

Half a million line
the barren promontory
watch the racers plodding by
to see for a brisk moment
the pain endured
to achieve the recorded narratives
one to maintain a place in the podium
after years away from glory
another seeking redemption
for the slight of the previous campaign
and two brothers in tandem
helping each other to the pinnacle

The thrill of the race holds him in its grip
three hours in the comfort of his seat
He grimaces and wonders
how much could he achieve to ride again
and climb no less a goal
than Mount Ventoux

Later he turns
to the books rescued from the shelf
of a newly opened second-hand store

Determined to read the first thing he finds
he reaches and pulls
The Canzoniere and Other Words
and opens to a random page

"Today I climbed the highest mountain in this region
which is not improperly called *Ventosum* (windy)
The only motive for my ascent was
the wish to see what so great a height had to offer"

He stops and reads again
searching for clues
Surely not the same Ventoux
but the introduction sets him right
Two brothers on a day
seven hundred years removed
on impulse resolve to climb Ventosum
One seeking the easiest passage
edges away from the top
winding along the sides
only to double back
to the straighter path the other offers
And when finally at the summit
he measures the distance and pulls
a book from his pocket
perhaps no larger
than what he holds now in his hand
and resolves to read the first lines
his eyes come upon

"And men go about admiring the high mountains
And the mighty waves of the sea
And the wide sweep of rivers and the sound of oceans
And the movement of the stars
But they themselves abandon"

He measures the consequence of what
seven hundred years have wrought

to put him on Mount Ventoux
and impose on him a book
that ponders a question
time has begun to ask of him

3) Dust in the Corners

He draws the curtains back
shakes the wooden shutters
that shelter the bay window
darts his eyes between the slats
back and forth across the rushing street

A bright sun holds the sky in its grip
rays cascade in ribbons
bounce colors wildly off window panes
and the set faces of strangers on the walk
The measured steps of shaped leather
scrape hard off worn stones
brakes grind voices rise
dogs bark masses jostle and cajole

Hard at the window his body sways to see
the way a day dissolves the mime of lights
that reflect off the street onto the glass
and the gray faces

With the full weight of his body
pressed against the jamb of the oak trim
he stands ready to draw the lace shears
to reveal the dust and webs
gathered at the corners
of the collapsing window frames

4) She Weaves the Shirt

While she weaves
the purple *buganvillas*
on the front of the white cotton shirt
a delicate task handed down
from mother to mother
since the days when the cloth
of her village was worth more than
the gold that drove the Spaniards mad

in another room his mother
strips the blood orange sun
from the heads of the zucchini
and sprinkles the *calabaza* blossoms
over the thick slurry of *frijoles* and pork
layered with soft *Oaxacan* cheese
and folds the corn *tortillas*
before laying them on the hot *comal*

as his sister takes the bloom
from roses big as fists
careful to pull each one apart
until they cover the table
where she squeezes them
and extracts the essence
rubs it into the folds of the plump hens
before she bakes them in the stone oven

as his aunt plucks the orange petals
floating in the cold water
mixes them with sugar and flour
molds the strands of dough
and shapes the *roscas de reyes*
that she will take to the stall
at the edge of the *zocalo*

He sits on the rugs he wove
from dawn to dusk and back
displaying the *tortas*
while sipping lemon grass tea
with sage honey
as she weaves the fragile petals
on the last shirt she will ever make

5) *Enrique Calderon Painted Pictures*

Enrique Calderon was always there
close to the edge out of the way
in the cafés bars and restaurants
shacks shanties and tents that sprang
along the dusty roads and rail yards
Enrique Calderon mixed his paints
with dust he collected from the cast-off
workers loiterers vagabonds
misfits and fathers that filed out
passed by shuffled in ambled up to
or ran past at closing opening hoping time
He put the colors in jars
labeling each carefully
Sunday Spring April 1935
Okie red from overalls in overturned car
Wednesday Summer August 1938
boxcar off the tracks brown
Thursday Fall November 1934
lost in desert medicine man turquoise
Tuesday Winter December 1936
Red River chalk from sunken boat
Saturday Spring 1936
uranium mine blue dust on baby rattle
Monday Spring May 1937
spring picker mustard yellow pollen fleece

Enrique Calderon painted large canvases
until they filled his space leaving
no place to unfold his bed roll
Then he painted smaller until
the canvas seams bulged
He became a conceptualist
filling his mind with finished works
In his dreams he stole into museums
and hung them on the walls

Enrique Calderon began painting portraits
trading them for breakfast lunch or dinner
Going from one town to the next
he painted until he walked
off the edge of the world

6) His Descent Is a Casual Thing

A feather
separated from a wren
knocked off its flight by a hawk
falls and rises
from one ledge to another
Tossed by updrafts and shears
it twists and glides along
the canyons of the city
Then a staccato fugue
a taut gust nudges it
against the façade
of the glass box
where it catches
the edge of a steel band
The afternoon breezes tease it
back and forth across the pane
as a cat in a glass room
swats and chases it

A distant murmur
announces the fall
A sudden blast of wind
grows to a roar
that sweeps the trees aside
buffets the glass
until a strong gust
pulls the quill
from the steel sheathing
It arcs from the glass
swirls a dizzy dervish
that draws an occasional glance
as it glides downward
a quivering arrow
awkward into
the thick soft grass

Chapter II
Border Crossings

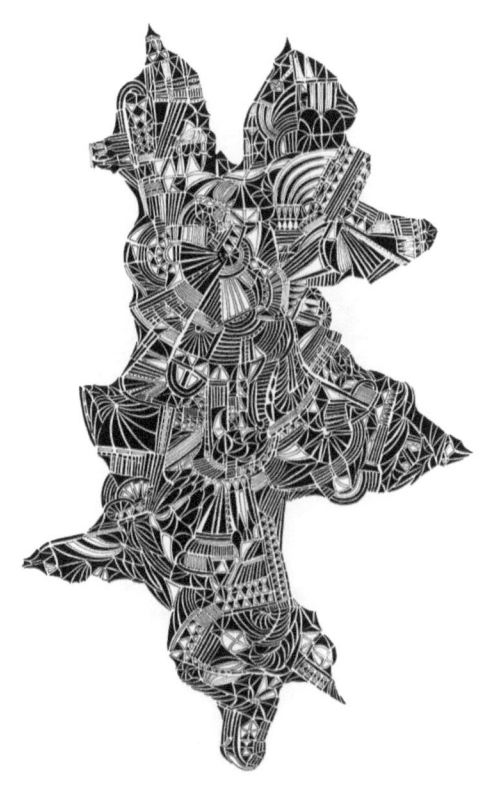

7) Border Crossings

Their spirits walked across the plains
rivers hills and mountain ranges
along ancient paths carved by roaming herds
heading south farther from winter's snow and ice
A carved line defiles the Badlands
as ashes in distant fires range
along the banks of the Platte and Colorado
fire-rings beneath the shelter of rock overhangs
or in the opening of caves above the winding rapids
or water flowing south deadly along the arroyos
canyons and valleys tracking
with the flocks and the seasons
Torn vestment strands long-since turned to dust
and carried along like the whispers
of faces around a communal fire
with songs flicking in the air like lightning bugs
the crackling embers of brush mesquite
aspens oaks walnuts sentinels

A whistle resonates across the desert
and rustles the wide grass of the plains
howls along the ridge of mountains
wakes spirits
the bridge and the way
to that home beyond the four corners
The elders carried it in suede pouches
and blessed the path with sage and oils
The old women built monuments of stones
marked the brown and red earth
that seeped through veins into the heart
the tracks of buffalo and boar
puffs of dust signposts for the return

Many migrations south till the histories
reside in the chants of *curanderas*

and the dance of shamans and elders
the detritus of peoples on the move
swallowed whole to disappear
into a memory instinct
a pale reminder of a path back
to the beginning
to the womb
to the mother land

A squat thick-chested brown man
walks along a river valley heading north
His eyes cast downward
to the dirt and rock beneath his feet
He studies the topography in blinks
Now and then he stoops
gathers rocks and pebbles
mounts them on top of each other
recreates the sturdy towers
no more than a foot off the dirt
He reconstructs the ancient highways
He is the indigenous returning to the land

8) Family Portrait

Mi familia stands facing the camera
from *mi abuela* to *mi prima* Leanor
and *tio* Guillermo to *mi tia* Emerita
framing the line that hugs close to the wall
Us kids are entwined and woven into the legs
elbows and waists of assorted other *tias* and *tios*

We are varying shades and tints
pink flushed cheeks next to olive brown arms
questioning ebony eyes beneath jet black curls
deep brown folds embracing plump peach cheeks

A bashful white face beneath golden braids grins
at *mi primo* Rafael's twisted face
as he succeeds in spoiling the decorum
of the family portrait

Then the stern look of *mi abuelita*
as she eyes the children that any moment
threaten to spill across the polished floor
like a stew about to overflow the boiling pot
as if with one look she can hold us back
in the container in the very pan
that has stirred our different flavors
into this mix of savory Creole *mestizo* Moor
from the sands of Arabia and the broad stretch of Africa
and the spreading tubers of *Al-Andalus*
La Extremadura and *Catalunya*
and the indigenous migrants from the north
and the bridge to the ancestral lands
to the mother to the patria
to the folds of the rift valley

We simmer and the bubbles subside for an instant
until the hand with the camera gives a thumbs up

and then this stew spills across the floor
to the door to the streets to the city
to the hills to the sea
to the discomfort of those who fail to see
the varying tones and tints
of our rapidly growing family

9) I Remember Jackson Mississippi

I know why
there are things I know
I am meant to know
It is a long trip
through the south of 1965
in a 1956 Chevy
My brother and I in the back
My mother stepfather in the front
and he is telling us something
She nods with tears in her eyes
but he is telling me the gospel truth
There are people in this place that will see
and not like the color of your skin
I remember clear as night
the sign *Jackson*
He points and teaches me to say
Jackson Jackson
One of my first words in English

I remember when I dated her
blonde hair and grey eyes
I would visit up north outside St. Joe
and lounge in her sister's yard
in the burning afternoon sun
The end of summer we broke up
Later she told me how relieved
her sisters-in-law were
to not have to drive by the house
and see the nigger on the lawn

When we lived in the suburbs
I had a friend who hated the lawn ornaments
that dotted his neighbors' yards
black jockeys holding reins in their hands
When I stayed the night we would get high

and run out into the dark
smashing the sculptures with our bats
A fungo to the head is as good
as any swing on cowhide
Some of the houses
replaced them with other jockeys
but through the years we saw them disappear
replaced by gnomes toads and deer

I think of that trip and know
what I am meant to know
three months after the bodies have been found
Cheney Goodman and Schwemer
in Neshoba County Mississippi
It has been forty-five years since I learned
Jackson and why he made me repeat it
until it flowed like venom from my tongue
I understand why she cried
and why I got such joy from
smacking the heads off the lawn jockeys
and watching them tumble
and bounce lazy across the lawns

10) The Old House on the Line

The kudzu sheaths
trees and bushes
A powder blue blanket
wraps around poles
that creep close to the edge
of a winding road

The asphalt buckles
Gravel spills across curves
and gathers in the folds
of quilts bunched
around two swinging gates
tethered open
eight feet on each side
of a narrow road

Wild grass nibbles at grey metal
earth laps over the bottom rails
angles into dirt
and swallows a comforter
long since become a bed for weeds

Some remnants
flap out of reach
of a collapsed porch
Two tattered pillowcases
and a fitted sheet
wind-ripped hang twisted
choked by rusting coils
of pins that once held
the bed firm on the line

Another comforter and shams
muffle the bang of the screen door
and trail along the fallen hall

that leads to a bedroom
where mattresses cough cotton balls
that flow out to the yard
through rotted checkered walls

Two rusted bedsprings
teeter totter
atop a stone wall
while wisps of down
swirl and whirlpool
in fluff tornadoes
to catch on the branches
of an old catalpa
slowly tilting down to the roots
and the kudzu that begins
to wrap about the house

Chapter III
This Is Tango

11) *This Is Tango*

El negro Casimiro
el mulato Sinforos
el Pardor midwives
at the birth of *Tango*

Likewise *el Flaco* Saul
la Parda Refucilo
Papa La Chata
and *la Mondonguito*
the head of the reptile

Tango snakes from the docks
the dancehalls and brothels
The reptile is chameleon
The snake is a *milonga*

Tango is a woman and a man
a hand held high
an arm about a shoulder
another at the back
The man leads
the woman follows
Tango is a sorrowful thought
that must be danced

Feel the blood rise
to your face with every beat
while an arm winds like a snake
around a waist
about to break

Tango is a song
Tango is a dance
It is the street
and the *barrio*

It is the place one leaves
and spends a lifetime
returning to

12) How Strange the Night

In the corner
in the space between
dusk and dawn
I take notice of your body
silent by my side

My trembling fingers
touch the mirror of your back
and I reach for
what the night conspires to deny
In that instant I feel
the thinness of my dreams

How strange the night
revealing much
and nothing

13) In the Bay

Voices on the bank
heave wreaths to the crests
while curtains tat about the panes
gauze dances out the open windows

The wind takes the boat
Waves ripple beneath it
My hand hard on the till
your face to the wind

Unattached
empty of each other
we bob and bide our time
long to lay our anchor
on a green certainty

14) One

We glide no more
than a foot above the glass
a fast moving
tandem silhouette

The point glides
and flaps its wings
A beat behind
the other flaps
and flaps an extra beat

A measured separation
off by one beat

15) *I Enjoy*

I enjoy the world swaying
to the demands of age-old scripts
content to lie for hours
with one leg over the other
mimicking the lazy rhythms
of sheltered waves lapping up the beach

Nothing bores her more than to see
a languid ocean spent
miles before it hits the bank

"Give me the roar and crash of water
over the rippled wake
of an indifferent wave"

I have watched the ocean wither
from a high crag after the sun dissolves
the evening fog creeping to the hills
like waves of tumbling smoke
slowly devouring the world

She longs for the cries of wild animals
ahead of raging fires turning tinder
all the brush and growth till speckles
flicker dangerous along a valley floor

I know the desolation
when a leaf descends
after a long journey
from a branch silent
into the still water of a cove
sending ripples
that grow larger to disappear
in the wake of other ripples
stirred by idle winds across

the mirrored surface of a lake

She is alive in raucous winds
that pummel trees and send leaves
crashing to the air tossed waters
She breathes the hard gusts of hurricanes
lashes her self to rocking redwoods

I linger at the edges of hillsides
sweeping up to high mountain meadows
sleep on the loam of purple orange columbines
stitched like a ruffle below the tree line

She rides the rush of water
from snow melts charging
gouging the face of mountains

"Let me jump from glacial tossed boulders
to volcano spewed rocks
and balance at the side of sheer drops
thousands of feet from the hard ground
Give me earth shaking
and rumbling ash spewing hilltops
and you show me the true nature of things"

I sit at the edge of hills
pray to condors eagles and hawks
riding thermals to the top
and laugh at the play of bear cubs
on the folding ridges of the high country

She marvels at the frenzy of bears
taking salmon from streams in big swipes
that turn the waters redder than her hair

I sit and wait beneath a warm moon
feel the heat like whispers on my skin
as the waves cascade in a dull distant snore

and I know that come tomorrow
the world will be mine in the hollow imprint
of a sole where I walked before I turned
and took the time to lay my blanket on the sand

16) She Is Late Returning

She is late
returning from the garden
taken by the violet of the aster
and the mums beneath
straining in the cool morning
The cannas get
some of her attention
more than the hibiscus
or the begonias
throwing off their orange
on the staggered steps
The gladiolas
dropping their last
merit her caress
but the bees and wasps
have their say
and she gives way

She does not know why
she has not cut down the weed
It grows fast and promises blooms
Certain a wild flower from the hills
has made a pilgrimage to her plot
She lets it grow its way
long after she knows
it is just a weed
She likes the shape

She comes retiring
reticent
sees the shutters swing
the soft and bony fingers
resting
on the weathered sill
the shoulders

warm and heavy
in the thick morning sweater
the head straining
above the turtleneck

Her eyes look up and catch
the gnarled trunk of the ivy
matted against stone walls
rising to enclose the house
She sees the toast on the table
and the jar of preserves
through the crook of his arm
and the fire in the hearth

She does not know why
she likes the shape
Still she finds a reason
to enter and share a cup

17) Today

She has taken the best of me
put it on the shelf
right of the picture window
in a glass half-filled
In the evening she will take
the suds from the dishwater
flick them on the rim
to stir swirl and tempest
to the bottom of the sill
In the morning she will rush
to see the best of me
drowned clawless drifting
across the ground sand

18) *Amor*

Amor saunters by
Her heels rasp across the walk
Ice pools at my door

Beads around her neck
Braided flowers left from spring
Drizzle will be snow

Sweeter than any berry
Fresh picked from the vine
I bring one a day

Hawks and ladybugs
Soar high in the morning sun
Leaves glide to the ground

Amor's smile beckons
Flip of the skirt entices
Slippery when met

The bright sun above
Shadowed by the pale moonlight
Many days follow

19) Rain Will Come What May

In my love's garden
When the ground is coarse and dry
Gardeners will not plant

Ladybugs and angels
Shout the only verities
Daisies will not bloom

But in the dim hope
That a flower will grow true
Is water essential

Saguaros bear fruit
In the desert and grow tall
Feel no hint of rain

Patient by nature
Blissful in the sun they grow
Rain will come what may

20) You Woke Me

You woke me this morning with your smile
arriving from the other side of the world
where ships barely dare navigate
The sailors used to long distances
rested by the side of the bed
while sands and diamonds
illuminated your smile

You woke me this morning with your caress
distant from my body long consoled
by the rough and crumpled blanket
and a mantle of thorns
You lulled my scream
with the light of the compass rose
and the pearls of your caress

You woke me this morning with your grace
full in your lips and kisses
and the curl of your fingers
Like Lazarus I awoke
relieved from the years
that lay heavy but now are
turned ash by the rays of your grace

21) When the Wind Is Slight

When the wind is slight and cool
the birds full about the feeders
and the seed plentiful
it overflows
and the squirrels gather
to grouse about

And the buds just formed
begin to leaf into a fullness
that obscures the branches
the grass high enough
to catch the early morning breeze
and the silence that comes over the hills
settles over the houses of the city

She will sit quietly at my side
sipping her coffee
with the morning paper
on her lap
and it will feel
like everything fits
the light sweater
the spring morning air
the trace of the sun
that lazy
burns away the fog
Yet it will come
crawling beneath the grass
burrowing close to my feet
a thin finger scratching
at the tips of my toes
a coldness creeping
up the tightening calves
slipping into the bones
coursing up my crooked back

reaching to the nape
beginning a massage
that steals my breath

And in the garden
in the breeze that flips
the pages easy
on my lover's knees
I become bones in a chair
with the worms
blithely crawling at my feet
What is the matter
she will ask
Nothing
I will tell her
There must have been
a hint of winter
in this early spring air
And I will close my eyes
and wait
the nothing I know is always there

Chapter IV
At the Water's Edge

22) *At the Water's Edge*

You wonder why they come
from so far away
to walk along the edge
I have wondered too
my back to the ground
my feet sinking in the sand
the water inching to my toes

And it comes to me
how young I was
before I saw the sea

I remember sun and wind
and her screams above the foam
I see the roll wrap itself
along the wide reach of my eyes
I see the glint just at my feet
after the water's rinse

I chase it
as it rolls and tumbles
on the tossed floor
I reach it
as her screams and waves embrace
somewhere above my head

I hold it just before
tumbled broken rinsed and spewed
twirling across the sand
and my empty outstretched hand

For years I tell her
I held a piece of gold tight
For years she tells me
we are never so blessed

as to lose the things
we have left behind
or to survive clean
the water's determined rinse

23) In the Simplest of Ways

At *Saqharra* you crossed my path
walking along the causeway
out of the columned halls
the black veil across your mouth
the length of your shadow
as it brushed against my knee

You walked onto the portico
outside Olympic House
You came on a breeze
The dates lost some of their leaves
You picked the *buganvilla*
tucked it to your hair

On the boat from *Piraeus* to *Siros*
with the setting sun
on the temple of Poseidon
you stood at the rail
with the sun cast halos
the wind's smooth caress

It was you on a white horse
crossed the *Ponte Vecchio*
with the half turned smile
of a girl retreating to a dream
While lovers stole their kisses
I held the reins for the king

Off the *Place de la Concorde*
on the darkened street
with speeding cars between
you stood and looked at me
then twirled and twirled and
dissolved into the rushing lights

It was you in your hand
the curl of your fingers
the smile that drew me to the bench
Sitting beneath O'Higgins' statue
my eyes to the pockmarked stones
while mimes told the news

It was you at *La Recoleta*
darting out of the mausoleums
a cat in your hands
Evita's flowers in your teeth
You danced the tango
while I sat quiet in my seat

In the vaulted cathedral
your brown smile is wide
in the flicker of the candles
as I lazy
in a hammock
by the bay
by the cliffs
falling to the sea
hope to meet you again
in the simplest of ways

24) There Is Nothing To Be Found

A corpse
a shoe
the hem of a skirt
the trace of a smile
the squeeze of a hand
one breath and the closing of a door

A photograph
too many and not one
a soul
a purple aster
withered in a smoked glass vase

Your hand scratching
slowly down my back
no back
no rolling onto you
no falling on the floor
or the cascade of pillows
beneath the fan
or the rustle of the sheets

A gust of heather
the clacking of a shoe
once only
The rustle of the bags
too many and not one
or the half skips and
clucks across the floor
The plié and pirouette to a stop
with the hands thrust to the side

There is nothing to be found
No pirouettes across the floor
No pirouettes across
No pirouettes at all

25) *The Water Moves In Circles about My Speech*

We launch canoes of birch
and willow seats oak paddles
with ochres and reds
painted on the sides

A measured humming into the water

The flowing ribbon of the stream
gray and silver
slow and winding

The wind sifts through the trees
a plaintive whistle out into the cold
Far above other winds move
thermals rising from the springs

Hawks and eagles soar
in escalator moments
high and easy to the sky

The buzzards hover
float to the branches
and quiet note the passing

A hawk moves
along the water's edge
from Washington to Hermann
past New Haven

We edge the prow
closer to the bank
In the hollow of a sandbar
build a fire
dim against the stars

We ease catfish
and cornbread crumble
gentle into the grease

The darkening wraps about our dreams
I grasp the blanket tighter
curling our bodies deep into the folds
the valleys rills and springs
and the folding hills
a crumpled comforter
bunched on a stiff mattress

The flowing ribbon of the river
gray and silver
slow and winding

Through the night
the drops steady hard
against the matted ground
puddles breach the mounds
sandbars shift till
constant in their
inconstancy

We curse the mud
make our way to shore
On the banks
with the houses
high on stilts
with dogs barking
we watch water
wrap about the land
separate banks into islands
and fields gray to the edge
The logs that raged
through the night
on the banks
crash and whittle

See
the boats labor in the eddies
fret into the currents
barges cut and strewn
across diminished lawns
docks floating just
above the rippled edges
The piles that gouge
pout into the river
The hills above the roots
dig deep into the dirt
release the red earth
into the rushing water

See
trunks tossed like oak barrels
across widening banks
as the water hazes
wrapping memory in lace

The raging ribbon of the river
gray and silver
slow and grinding

See
rotting hulks of houses
cars leaching
poison to the ground
as hands rush to the water's edge
once more for cleansing

See
flocks of geese migrate
slow down the careening edge
They will be late arriving
Somewhere horses thunder
distant on the hills

Rabbits and squirrels stop
see the naked season
surrender quickly
seek to burrow deeper
into other basements
cellars and coffins

There is nothing in passing
and leaving is just
the movement from one
moment to another with
no trace of embarrassment

The sun blinks across the sky
Water pools become
drizzles in the afternoons
With the first nights come
redbirds and flags
waving in the air

The whistle of the train
marks the distance
from the small bedrooms
side by side along the track
to the glow of bodies
warm and safe
the evening's new arrivals
huddled inside fires
raging in a flooded square

Around a leafless standing oak
pictures and letters
and curios on a shelf
form floes and oxbows
break the shelter
shunt the storm

And everywhere
the land's acceptance
and the rolling over

New rivers and streams will flow
and when time has reclaimed us
we won't see the stitching
the rocks witnessing
the defiles into the earth

We won't cross the wideness
that stretches into miles
will not watch the flocks
fly tire and rest
when they reach
the other side

We walk to opposite shores
The train whistle us away
The whining at the curbs
signaling moments
things left so far behind
in a diary burning in the light
above the flattened homes
that shape the air
and slam the winds
past stones that frame
the bulging hillocks
and the cut wild grasses
tamed to a height
that barely touches
the playful breezes
You follow the bent signposts
hidden meanings and designs
Ride along the byways
the divined destination

I let trains carry me to the plains
away from the cliffs and water
I go to where the rhythms
long since gave way
to beats bangs regrets

The flowing ribbon of the stream
gray and silver
slow and winding

You embrace wind sun
and folded horizons
Tumble roll and wrinkle
like an unfolding towel
weaving a gypsy symmetry
and I vagabond
once removed
from the bank

I take make
incomplete sentences
like faded orange balls
strung across power lines
where a bridge once spanned
from one shore to another
to ask
what would I
do if once more found
below a blood red moon
in a high season
with the waters
coursing over the dikes
and the full train stations
the locomotive's whistle
silent across the folded fields
and the waters that move
in circles about my speech

26) Why I Don't Sing

In an instant
I saw you disappear
You became a figment
an accident
of arrival or departure

I pretended to see you grow
through etched mirrors
You
a student of music
I
a failed mural painter
years before I touched a brush

I remember good bye
wild-eyed and tussle-haired
your hands in my pockets
your teeth tight
till the gums bled
into your thirsty mouth

Any moment I feared
your mouth would open
and bathe this desert

When you started singing
I slipped into the café
a crowd gathered
and I lost my way

The absence of you
finds me
an unconnected leaf
dropped from branch
cut from root

expelled from seed
faded
colorless to earth

Don't come back now
to see the lines
the years have etched on my face
to see the pounds
the fears have grafted about my waist

I have not been a painter of life
Life has made me its canvas
and I begin to peel
watch the color fade

I who always sang off-key
heard you singing
in the street
and slipped away

27) *Baile*

La calaca came knocking on my door
like so many other times before
I do not see her hiding in the bushes
As I turn back into the living room
her bony legs trip me
and I land on the floor
I love it when that happens
She laughs as she heads for the altar
and helps herself
to the *ofrendas* on the shelf
Hey what gives *señorita*
You know these are for the souls
that will come tomorrow night
Do you really think I am a *señorita*
She smiles coyly
the blush coloring her bleached bones
Of course my lovely
And for the umpteenth time
since we first met
I lead her to the table
and serve her *tamales*
baked in banana leaves
a tall glass of *avena*
with a hint of cinnamon
On the stove *arroz con pollo*
spiced with cloves and
littered with green olives simmers
I pour her a cup of *vino de casa*
and in the candlelight we reminisce
Tio Jaime and *tu primo* Sancho
send their regrets
Emerita *tu abuelita*
cries over her *cuco*
Give me a picture to take to her
Then she takes a finger

and slowly strokes my beard
and with the hollow of her eyes
looks deep into my heart
You know someday I will come for you
Don't think of work tonight my dear
I reach behind her on the table
and pull the long stem rose
She puts it in her mouth and stands apace
I push the player to shuffle
and in a tight embrace we sway
to *boleros* and *tangos*
the rattle of her bones an eerie metronome
I ply her with wine and sweet nothings
She is tipsy in my arms
I feel she will fall asleep
but she glides awkward across the floor
stops and plucks the rose from her mouth
These advances are so nice
to feel and be what I was once
but it is futile to resist
Someday I will come for you
and what will have been the point of this
Nada chica nada
but you can't blame me for trying
Besides how many guys can claim
to have danced with such a lovely death
cheek to cheek in a tight embrace
Alma de mi vida
you can really *shake and bake*

Chapter V
José Calderon Speaks

28) When I Talk

I don't want to be old
tired
stretched
useless
a frayed belt
a silent record

I want to shout
not end up squeaking

Perhaps if I started over

Listen to me
Listen to me
When I walk
one step in front of the other
I spin the earth beneath me

Maybe I walk too fast
My feet don't grip
The earth stands still

29) Mood with No Face

An uninvited sadness
grips me and starts a quarrel
I have no strength to end

My heart beats quick enough
A sudden rush
and my body
in a moment swings

I am suspended

A pebble tossed
skipped across the water
skimming the surface

A moment
between flying and crashing
with the promise
of sinking and landing
dependent on nothing

30) Fall Is A Craving

The witch hazel sheds
a crackling cacophony
winter is certain

Hawks and eagles soar
past Hermann and New Haven
empty canoes float

Barnyard swallows fly
encrypt secrets to the sky
doors and shutters close

The bay is empty
women retreat to the hearth
ships leave on long trips

Amor's compass rose
fixes on a certainty
I steer by the stars

Gazing on the sky
ride the prime meridian
to the east or west

The constellations
constant in their constancy
are obscured by clouds

The vase on the sill
holds a wilted violet
a candle goes out

In a hallowed box
where carrion clings to bone
bloom forget-me-nots

Fall is a craving
that lingers long past winter
whispers trail behind

31) Ten Days Now without Rest

A *bandeneon*
a freeze-up *tango*
a sparse bar
an early night in *Buenos Aires*
A dark-haired girl swoons to the ground
A second from the floor a pull from a hand
a stiff turn and exit via the kitchen to mild applause

In the chairs an old couple sits patient
as the waiter pours the wine
Just wait the older ones do it so much better

I drink until the bottles are one
and memories rush over me
as they step to take the stage

A woman answers the door
in heels and a black lace gown
while Sinatra plays in the dark
A lover calls her name as she laughs at a boy
selling door to door brooms for the blind

A preacher and his wife invite me for dinner
put the White Album on the stereo box
This is the best one they have made he yells
as his dear wife becomes familiar
with the growing bulge above my knees
A girl sways easy on a bed to Kind of Blue
Ooh baby how you keep the mood with that tune

A girl on a beach in Brazil sends me a kiss
in the Noname Bar in *Ermoupoli*
She says *your girlfriend is very beautiful*
I say yours is too and we toast them both
while a turntable spins Getz on an island
a Homeric night between evening and dawn

In the mirrors she dances a freakish *Scheherazade*
skipping like a bouncing ball of yarn
another story of long nights in the corner of booths
in dim lit bars and quarters stacked on the table
Take them play any song you want
I got nothing but quarters tonight
and cigarettes sheets of paper and well oiled pens
I was in the corps at City Ballet she says to me
and now it is *Doctor Feelgood* and *Fever*
She sways her hips in the smoke to the clang of glasses
never quite empty never quite full
the price of admission high
the cost of attention prohibitive
No one notices as she does her last encore
in the back of a beat up jeep
and she takes me back
to chancel choir and Gregorian chants
and the penance for one bad note sung too many times

He takes her hand and moves across the weathered floor
while she closes her eyes and though he leads
she goes where she wants to go
At the kitchen door the young girl bites her lips
Her partner sips a drink and smirks
until a jab to his side from her elbow
turns him to see the tear that slides down her cheek

And somewhere in San Telmo
between the evening and dawn
an old couple and Gardel
prove the waiter right
The older ones do it so much better

32) Malvern Hill

The branches have dropped to the ground
heavy with the cold rain's bracelets

The stalls are closed
The wind whistles through the trestles
still in need of a fresh coat of paint
The hands that fumbled at the table
with the bread crumbs in her fingers
have disappeared

When I last saw her
she was riding a horse bareback
hard into the wind and the night

There goes a girl
with a particular affliction
She sleeps hard upon the pillows

I slough off to the only bed I know
the only familiar that wakens me

I
am not the I
not the I
that you would think

I
gather up the straw that falls about
and make whole a man with no reflection

I
set out to see the yesterdays
that passed me by
through the smoke
burning in the eyes

through the pages
littered on the floor
the messages not read
the calls not returned
the letters not sent
or written
or thought upon
or the ashtrays
overflowing on the dusty sill

And the door
that constant creak that sounds
only when I leave and enter
and the rug worn and bare
to the splintered floor
and the many layers of paint
fallen to the ground
among the papers that pile up
with the sameness of the toss
and the sameness
of the letters and the words
I am I
at the border
I
at the sides
I
at the rail
like a guilty witness to a murder

My death
a silent falling down
down to the crushing
bending of the legs
and the stiffness of the joints
cramped and crimped
till useless to the neighbors

I carry myself like a gentle man

with my white flowing hair
my face hard into the wind
disdainful of a cane
not a crutch to anyone
no help to anyone

No one waits for me
and I wait for no one

Except for her
that girl that fell
down the dried river bed
as she careened past the summer stalls
and gathered all the color
swept some into the folds of her apron
and tucked the rest neatly in her bonnet

She fell down into a hole
Her rose drawn cheeks
fixed their eyes on me
She yelled
help me please
you there
a crutch to no one
no help to anyone

I saw her fall
and no one came for her

I went no further
than the startled rush
of feathers in a swamp
at the falling of a pebble
into a shallow cove

I saw the crime and did not report it
Who would listen and to what would I relate
a girl tumbling rolling with summer stuffed

into a picnic basket and a pomegranate
in her hand

I know where she rests
but I will not go there
I am not a master of the arts
I am a blessed observer
and a quiet one at that

33) *This Town Like That*

Sometimes
this town reeks like
lilacs forsythias redbuds
tulips roses and irises
wet and green to the gills
Tomatoes potatoes
melons and squashes
finches jays purple martins
bluebirds cardinals hummingbirds
robins meadowlarks buntings
sparrows doves crows
titmice and bats

Summer dresses short skirts
wraps tight shorts
bare chests long walks
crowded promenades
sipped coffees iced drinks
park lunches weekend retreats
stolen kisses
shades cars laughs curses grins
porches grills meats smoke
drinks mixed until drunk
high shy wild and sly
winks enticements and lies
love hate family meals indigestion
graduations rituals songs
burps farts and kisses
girls boys holding hands
dates dancing singing shouting
caresses soothing embraces
forgiveness over and over again

Sometimes this town is like
yards crests hills and overlooked bluffs

pigs horses cows and ruts
patties pastures fields
punched holes curses remorse
bonfires raging across flood plains
torches air gray smoke sulfurous
chocked dimmed orange flakes
cracked hazed hung horizons
no lights no welcome candles
to the gates of hell

This town like nothing I know
nothing to know
This town like arms crossed
behind eased backsides
This town infectious viral
narcotic addicting
waiting to pounce

Water dirt gravel
asphalt cement ribbons
Long stretches of strangers
Bricks mortar glass wood veneers
expand flow roam to mulled yards
Trains always and lullaby trails
a pinch of pain hung in mid air
I don't want this town
be the last thing I see

This town is like
sleet snow dust ice storms
drizzle rains floods
hail tornadoes
thunder and lightning
wind sun drought fires

This town lingers like
promises winks nods
arguments taunts and refrains

greased palms neglect hucksters
chamber religious ordained
flags waving hymns swaying
exploding peonies
chrysanthemums willows
diadems palms crossettes
horsetails rings cherry bombs
Roman candles and cake

Low wages body spent
bus fares one-way transfers
districts enclaves and jails
dog parks locked fences
brats with wallets
urban remake pioneers
grafters and schills

This town like that sometimes
This town like any town most times
This town like a bur up my ass
like a bad dream like tripping
hallucinogenic
This town shimmers
like a star on a hill
I might not leave this town
This town may have left me
This town might be the death of me
This town plays me like that sometimes

34) What Was of Us

Imprinted on feathered pillows
down comforters and wool runners
opened green bare windows
reflections off fogged mirrors
slow lingered morning showers
black curls wound tight round a brush
and foam swirled about a jasmine bar

or camisoles careless on walnut bench
jewelry box neck laces clasped
jammed sideboard to wall
a hasp dangled open door
pitted and matted rugs
fixed to polished floors
brown heels and pumps
sandals a wayward sock
darned unraveled
greying strands

or faces in frames eye level
above pale withered asters
in dried crystal vases
looped forget-me-nots
rosewater traces on a sill
in halls shadowing bare spots
paint stains dripped
on quarter rounds
dust mottled tendril wisps
gathered bunched in the dark
of polished corner steps

couches covered rumpled sheets
glass tables watermarks
and fingerprints
letters magazines dusted plates

curios glass menageries encased
cards notes pencils
pitted silver candleholders
brass letter openers
crimson lipstick on the rim
wine crusted blood orange
a hand a paper and glasses
on a woven basket set
askew a maple table top

light streaming skipping
across marred shelves
and cabinet stalls
and reminders magnetized
to refrigerator doors
empty stained coffee cups
crumbs of sourdough

all of us in the margins
and the folded notices
yesterday's recycle
rotten maple and oak
mulched steps and hints of snow
as the silk rent
from your shawl
muffles the swinging door

35) I Was Mute

I open my mouth and am mute
A breeze blows in through a window
no scent attached
Sentinels huddled at the feeders
hum a curious pitch less drone
The water's flow
is neutral to my touch
I drink and do not
quench my thirst

The water runs overflows
spills and winds on the floor
seeps into the drain empties out the back
flows across the lawn to disappear
where the hawthorn grows
I cut my clothes through the hedge
and stand where the flow
runs to a bed of gravel
a faint scent and traces of a raspy tune
somewhere down the winding bed

I open my mouth and sentences tumble
knock one against the other
bounce spiral splinter
to syllables consonants broken phrases
crash to the gravel mix with the flow of water
disappear into the rock
the only hint
a dunning shadow
spreads from the edge
an oval along the gravel bed
I step in and follow
Soon cascades of words empty
from culverts and drains
as words turning to letters

dash against rocks turning to pebbles
The flow rages along the narrow stream
that digs deeper to the earth
Sentences dashed against the gravel
lose their veneer and letters their pretense
Caught in the torrent
they tumble to be devoured
by a tree shrouded cove
silence
and a crown of hyacinths

At the farthest reach
on a branch that anchors to a clear pool
shaded from the blazing sun
dipping its hooked beak
into a spout of letters gurgling up
through the filters of the pebbles
sits a hyacinth Macaw
gnawing the spent vowels
churning chewing and chattering
a melodious rasping squawk

Chapter VI
Bitter Suite

36) Bitter Suite

Fall is a hunger
that lingers
long past winter

I.
The canopies are strewn about
The squirrels in a mad dash
gather and hide
what in a few days
they will have forgotten
Then they will sit and wait
for the seed that fills the feeders

The winds have changed
In the morning
the briskness cuts
easy through the fabric
and with its fingers
trails across my back
I see the wind play its games
I see it run squirrel
and shake the leaves and dry branches
to the ground
It soars up the naked trunks
and slaps the tops
It sends sparrows and ravens
down into the shelter
of the creaking barn
In the swaying afternoon
the grayness of night approaching
it drops a shower of rotting leaves
to cascade about my feet
It gathers itself and lurks
at the edges of the woods
and in a sudden rush

embraces me
Take me

It only snaps its tail
across my face and leaves
laughing as it winds up the trunks
and tickles the remaining leaves
on the balding crowns
It jumps down to the lower branches
hugging from lesser trunk
to lesser trunk
It is a smile on the naked redbuds
as it tweaks the tips
Then it is gone
a tumble of leaves
spiraling along the ground

In the stillness
the sun fades in lazy fits
and lights the droplets
falling random upon my cheeks

II.
Out of the garden
the patch and the orchard
Past the gate
firmly set in the brick
cold wind and rain
take me step and step
Another gate another space
a path that wends
back upon itself

See the stone on the ground
The stone lies heavy on the plot
Lift up the stone
Call it here
Bring it easy

Find the notes
Something will move it
I will sing and it will fly

Graceful is the flight of the stone
Singing lift all the other stones
Stack them one on top of another
Watch the notes bend and resonate
Stones like figure eights
bouncing along the taut lines

The air is still
Still
The air is still

III.
Think to the middle
of a cool breeze blowing
gentle across the face
of a girl with flowers in her hair
She dreams of temples in the air
She turns to me
Who are you
I am a builder of temples in the air
In the still air
Girl turn to me
Girl turn to me as I sing
See
An edge forms here
Nothing tumbles here
The stones that form the edge
have made our bed
Come lie with me
Wait nothing
think nothing
but the grace of a song
on a wave of air stirring
the building of an altar

a temple in the air

Come here girl let us dance
you on that corner and me here
Twirl twirl and twirl
turn to me your eyes
and your darkening hair
Open your arms
I will come to you
You make the first move
I will make the last

Open up
The air is moving
stones are flying
The sweat that forms about my brow
drips drips slow
rivulets upon the ground

You turn and catch my eye
                Give it back
You turn and catch my breath
                Give it back
My heart tumbles to your feet
                Give it back

At the corner
the movement of your skirt
the turn of your heels
high in the air
                Give it back

The brush of your lashes
across my cheeks
The taste of your berry tongue
upon my lips
                Give it back
                Give it back

IV.
Falling into your eyes
I kiss your lips
and out into the silent streets
my sonorous voice
joyous above the multitudes
gathered in silent pews

I sing to the rafters
Stones fly with me
Sparrows sing canary

I am scale melody and counterpoint
joy in the upper and lower registers
a bridge affirming
a coda
I am dissonance and consonance
in a communal choir
I am chaos harmonious
The period to a raging storm
I am tamer of winds and wills
of days nights and dreams
As I am so is the world

I am the gift given
the gift accepted

V.
Fall is a hunger
that lingers
long past winter

I walk slow to the sound ahead of us
Are you there
so light in the back
Do I hear you in the path
Don't look back
The losing is in the looking

I am afraid of nonexistent
steps behind my shadow
Up ahead the light that is swelling
Behind
Barely a whisper
Are you there
Do you see me

I am a beard
grown gray on a worn face
in a tight room with drawn shades
lit by a candle
that flickers seconds away
above a Greek diner
that opens all night

And you so timid to others
a raging storm in my center
Strain for the light
I promise a world
The opening is here
the entrance waits

Are you there

VI.
The end of the day comes in the beginning
In the tick tick tick
of a counter reset and reset and reset
until a familiar smile breaks
on the corners of a drawn face
one that knows me but turns
afraid to take a step
And the day ends in the sun
on a park bench at noon
with pigeons huddled on bread crumbs
with the north wind
spitting gusts in the fall

as the leaves brown
Tick tick tick talk
The day ends in the shadows
of a face dissolving
with my arm about an aura
whose substance fades
to a caprice

I turn
turn
turn
slow to the anger that swells
Don't resign
I am not others
I am I
Take a chance girl
take a chance
Don't
turn
turn
turn away

VII.
Out of the garden
past the gate
firmly set in the brick
another space and other steps
steps that turn to themselves
and return to the start
that ends at the door
of a window that closes

Hear a laugh receding
like a love dreamt
See a woman alone
in the stillness passing
from today to tomorrow
inexorable

unattended
In the still air
the stones fall flat around the plot
and your name heavy and straight
is etched on the graying rock

VIII.
Tomorrow comes tonight
timid to the touch

There is nothing to be found
A corpse
a shoe
the hem of a skirt
The trace of a smile
The squeeze of a hand
One breath and the closing of a door

A photograph
Too many and not one
A soul
A purple aster
withered in a smoked glass vase

Your hand scratching
slowly down my back
No back
No rolling onto you
No falling on the floor
Or the cascade of pillows
beneath the fan
Or the rustle of the sheets

A gust of heather
and the clacking of a shoe
once only
The rustle of the bags
too many and not one

Or the half skips and
clucks across the floor
The plié and pirouette to a stop
with the hands thrust to the side
There is nothing to be found
No pirouettes across the floor
No pirouettes across
No pirouettes at all

IX.
Think of a memory
easily forgotten
Think of a tryst in a cold room
and the words not spoken
The long sleep furtively taken
The nights of hiding
and the passion of time
backwards
Back to the beginning
of a dull sensation in the groin
an ember that strains for the wind
that whistles above a scream in a closet
of walls caving and the urine
that hangs in the air
the legs bent and wound
tight to the stomach

Think of a hunger
that lingers
A malignant embrace
that attaches carrion
on a lifelong passage
A killing cure
a redemptive curse

Come boys here
melodies for the taking
Pick a name and I will extend it to night

and in your lover's arms you will awaken
Silly girls
all of a piece and for making
Don't promise what morning will change
You leave off better the one
that will embrace you tonight
than the one
that in the morning awaits you
Better in the arms
that barely embrace you
than the mood turned reverential
and the familial that kills you

I am craftsman
nothing defines me divine
I am a gift given a gift wasted
with no purpose no direction
set in the street with a power
that blinds me

X.
In the measure of a life
a string wends through the center
A careening nothing
ties strands into a knot
The night drinks
from the parched ground
I am thirsty
This is not a comfortable bed
It should face the courtyard
where the sun breaks
and in the dawn
frames the open window
In a moment there will be
pictures on the wall
music in the air
laughter on the floor
In a moment

there will be someone
out of the darkness
with their eyes wide
and he will say
Come follow me
again and again
In that moment
I will know you
know me

XI.

The red sun catches the spigot
as it drips a constant flow
that pools onto the muddy floor
The ravens flutter to the edge
and shake the drizzle
a raucous splash
in the waning afternoon

I step to the water's edge
and sink into the cool mud
I see the water that overflows the pool
trickle along the path
I step light
step by step
And as I walk along the path
that brings me from the bath
with my eyes on the rotting mulch
that fills the space between the logs
I find the berry with its red coat
buried in the folds of the ivy
I draw it to my mouth
I am struck by the bitter sweetness
Here in late fall a strawberry fruits
and dissolves behind my lips

Oh
Once

They called me the strawberry boy
and with my basket full
in the high measure
of a melodious spring
found me
wild
as the west wind
on the skin
certain
as the morning dew
on the lilac sprig
come to feed you strawberries
one by one
Sweet
as an expectant kiss

Do you hear them calling
Bring on the baskets boys
Here in this patch
there is plenty of fruit
Come boys
take them to your sweethearts
Put a strawberry to her mouth
Watch the fruit
disappear behind her lips
See the smile and the turn of the eyes
as they come to rest on you
Hear the lips
that mouth your name
Take another love
Take another love
Take another love
I bring a full basket

XII.
The wind at the edges
lurks and frets
and whips itself into a rage

It darts across the checkered cover
of the oaks and sycamores
and swirls into a tempest
on the flooding floor

The spigot
strains and breaks
The water
cascades in falls across the path
And the ground
bleeds berries
And I am a picker of berries
Another hand
and another handful
and the bosom of my shirt swells red
Wait love
wait
I gather
the first of this year's crop

XIII.
Age time and wind wither their histories
on the stones that litter the silent plots
In the shade of a day grown cold
a youth grown old
a flickering light disappearing
By the graying stones
akimbo on the fresh dead lawn
engulfed by the winds
that claw the swaying trunks

On a mound just off the path
that wends about
I sit and wait
with a full basket in my arms
If darkness
gives one more chance
find me here love

again and again
come back for you
until I get it right

Afterword
The Life and Times of José Calderon

37) *Epifania*

I.
Blue gray snow at the base of a fence
Black trees silhouette the top
On frozen branches
twelve cardinals huddle
A crimson pool
puddles from an open mouth
The shrieks and yelps
that filled the night
spun up by the gusts are
sprayed on the velvet ground

II.
Storylines in a musty paneled room
soft bindings in old books
dust in a spider's web
a walk
a half-step from the door
and the sheet on the floor

III.
I heard a song falling across the hills
exploding like a waking cicada in June

Song of retching masses
dying on veins of concrete
counting time by bolted back doors
of stiff fingers moving rocks
across cracked checkerboards
beneath buckling tenement walls
of reposing old men by an undying sea
of spring rains on green flowers
clutched by expectant brown fingers
from the lone hands of young women
of sun-weathered heroes riding

the crests of gargantuan waves
of young love
that pounds on immutable rocks
floods over frayed pictures
of first kisses and death
of one night stands hotels motels and epitaphs

I would I could have gone
where others went
I would I could have been
what others were
I would I could have seen
what others saw
I would I could have known
what others knew
I would I could have sung
what others sung
instead I turned and looked away

Mea culpa
Mea culpa
La culpa es mia

IV.
A hushed history
imagined
lived
written
in a three hundred
thousand word dictionary
In the margins
an address without numbers
sinks like a rock
between Apollo and Zeus
The innocent are guilty
The gods are not kind

38) Epilogue

Across the great divide

The wall goes up
along the southern front
while further down in
Michhuah's high sierra
the place of the fishermen
in the pine oak
and *oyamel* canopies
black and orange wings
drape stout branches
closer to the ground

Sated they sleep
until a day lengthens
the temperature rises
The hibernating roost stirs
spring's awakening
The longing of propagation
in chrysalides finds form
purpose metamorphosis
Nascent wings
take the first breeze
find north and leave
a flutter of a billion wings
like the whistle of a drizzle
a wet whispered goodbye
for the trip to El Norte

The guard posts along
the fence and nascent wall
a gouge of no consequence
The breezes blow the wings
obstacles are scaled with ease
The first hosts drop their eggs

and spread the commands
flutter and flutter north
The tumultuous states
hardly an impediment
to nature's whim

They flit about the banks
nest in sandbars along
forgotten river roads
and garden sanctuaries
of *salvia* Siberian wallflower
tithonia diversifolia
chives and *asclepias syriaca*
Their focus north
to the sap and nectars
of asters and goldenrod
yarrow prairie clover and ratibida
the summer's convening in full

The disappearing day
and coming chill signal
the southward retreat
imprinted millennia of migrations
back to Michhuah
an internal map
embedded compass
a primordial memory
a call back to the first
home and spread of wings
to fields of *cempazúchitl*
and the hum of *colibrí*
bonfires on the hills

In the trails behind
remembrance of the dead
the remnants broken
or pinned on plastic limbs
in cabinets with faux grass

inside a glass menagerie
a curiosity plastered
on a window shield
a corpus on a chalked walk
or the leaves of toxic guards
tales of sandbanks full
clusters of orange
crumpled like embers
a dead fire on a river bank
and the gasps of children
spent from chasing dreams
till another season
melancholic in repose
tossed and turned
signals the return

ACKNOWLEDGMENTS

"José Calderon Supposes" and "Malvern Hill" originally published in *Raritan: A Quarterly Review*, Spring 2014.

"I Remember Jackson Mississippi" originally published in *This Town Like That*. Kansas City, MO: Spartan Press, 2015.

"She Is Late Returning," "When The Wind Is Slight," "In The Simplest Of Ways," "The Water Moves in Circles about My Speech," and "Bitter Suite" originally published in *Primera Página: Poetry from the Latino Heartland*. Kansas City, MO: Cucui Press, 2008.

"At the Water's Edge" originally published in *I-70 Review*, Summer 2012.

"Family Portrait" originally published as "Retrato de Familia" in *Whirlybird Anthology of Kansas City Writers*. Shawnee, KS: Whirlybird Press, 2012.

"This Town Like That" published in chapbook *This Town Like That*.

José Faus, a Bogota, Colombia native and longtime Kansas City resident, is a founding member of the Latino Writers Collective and has been involved in many mural works in the Kansas City area, Mexico, and most recently Bolivia, where he received a cultural ambassador grant from the U.S. State Department. He is the 2011 winner of Poets & Writers Maureen Egen Writers Exchange award and maintains a studio practice at **caridostudio** in downtown Kansas City, KS.

www.ingramcontent.com/pod-product-compliance
Lightning Source LLC
Chambersburg PA
CBHW020619300426
44113CB00007B/712